# 5 SECRETS TO PROFITABLE SHRINK SLEEVES

## HOW MATERIALS & ARTWORK ARE CHANGING THE FACE OF BUSINESS

# 5 SECRETS TO PROFITABLE SHRINK SLEEVES

## HOW MATERIALS & ARTWORK ARE CHANGING THE FACE OF BUSINESS

Shubham Singhal

Worldwide Published by
**Pendown** Press

**PENDOWN PRESS LLP**
**An ISO 9001 & ISO 14001 Certified Co.,**
**Regd. Office:** 3767A, Kanhaiya Nagar,
Tri Nagar, Delhi-110035
**Ph.:** 8130886000, 9650072927
**E-mail:** info@pendownpress.com
**Branch Office:** 1A/2A, 20, Hari Sadan, Ansari Road,
Daryaganj, New Delhi-110002
**Ph.:** 011-45794768
**Website:** PendownPress.com

**Edition:** 2024
**Price:** ₹ 299
**ISBN:** 978-93-6338-086-8



*Layout and Cover Designed by* Pendown Graphics Team
*Printed and Bound in India by* Thomson Press India Ltd.

# Table Of Contents

# A Gift of Gratitude

**Mr. Akshar Yadav (AY)**

I want to express my heartfelt gratitude to all those who have supported me on my journey. First and foremost, I begin by thanking my mentor, AY, for guiding me and helping me understand my capabilities. His encouragement has been invaluable in establishing my name in the industry.

I am also deeply thankful to my parents and brothers for their unwavering support and belief in me. A special thank you goes to my wife, Pooja, for her love and encouragement throughout this process.

Lastly, I want to extend my sincere appreciation to Mr. Deepak Pawar whose motivation inspired me to write this book. Your support has made a significant difference in my journey, and I am truly grateful.

# *Wondering if this Book is for you*

If you are from the packaging industry, this book is definitely for you!

This book is designed to be an essential resource for anyone involved in the packaging industry, particularly those working with shrink sleeves. Irrespective of whether you have a lot of experience or are just starting out, you'll find this book packed with valuable insights practical knowledge, and tips tailored to your needs.

**So, Who Can Benefit from This Book?**

1. **Packaging Professionals:** If you're involved in the creation, design, or manufacturing of packaging materials, particularly plastic-based solutions, this book is a must-have. It will help you understand how to best utilize shrink sleeves in your packaging strategies and offer tips on improving your processes, designs, and material choices.

2. **Producers of Plastic and Shrink Sleeve Materials:** This book is highly relevant for companies and professionals involved in manufacturing plastic materials, shrink sleeves, or labels. Whether you're looking to innovate, improve product quality, or streamline production methods, the book offers technical details, emerging trends, and best practices.

3. **Label Manufacturers:** For those in the business of creating shrink sleeve labels, this book provides industry insights, covering everything from label design to material performance. It will guide you on how to optimize your labels for better branding, shelf appeal, and functionality.

4. **Students and Newcomers:** If you're studying packaging, materials engineering, or any related field, or you're simply new to the industry, this book will serve as an excellent guide. It simplifies core concepts, making it easier for you to grasp key principles and the latest advancements in shrink-sleeve technology.

**Business Leaders and Decision Makers in FMCG Companies:** CEOs, business owners, procurement managers, and heads of packaging in fast-moving consumer goods (FMCG) companies will find this book valuable. Shrink sleeves play a crucial role in the visual presentation and protection of your products. Understanding the technicalities of this packaging solution can help make better decisions about procurement, packaging strategies, and product presentation.

# *What Can I Promise You?*

I promise you that after reading this book, you will be empowered with the essential knowledge and confidence to make the right choices when buying shrink sleeves. I promise that you won't end up with the wrong product, which can lead to costly mistakes and problems in your supply chain, brand reputation, and overall market presence.

By following the insights and expert advice shared in this book, you will protect your business from the potential damage that many companies face when navigating the complex world of packaging. Instead, you will pave the way for success.

You can expect to see profit and growth as a result of selecting the right products and services tailored to your needs. My commitment is to help you navigate the packaging industry effectively, ensuring that your decisions lead to positive outcomes for your business through strengthening your brand, improving efficiency, and fostering growth. You can achieve a brighter future for your brand.

## How Will This Book Help You?

This book is designed to help you avoid the common challenges that come with poor packaging choices, which can result in waste, financial loss, and missed opportunities in a competitive market.

Whether you're a business owner, a packaging professional, or a procurement manager, you'll discover the tools you need to understand the technical aspects of shrink sleeves, how to choose the right materials, and how to ensure compatibility with your product lines.

With this understanding, you'll be able to make purchasing decisions with full confidence, knowing that you've selected the best packaging solutions suited to your specific business needs.

By applying the knowledge and strategies shared in this book, you'll not only prevent potential problems but also leverage your packaging strategy to enhance your brand's visibility, appeal, and performance in the market.

## What Can You Expect?

By following the recommendations and practices outlined here, you will —

➢ **Minimize Risk:** You'll avoid the costly mistakes of choosing incorrect or substandard shrink sleeve materials, ensuring your packaging consistently meets the highest quality standards.

➢ **Strengthen Brand Identity**: Properly selected shrink sleeves can elevate the look and feel of your product on the shelf, leading to greater consumer appeal and loyalty.

➢ **Enhance Operational Efficiency**: With the right products in hand, your supply chain will run smoothly, avoiding production delays or packaging failures that could disrupt distribution or lead to recalls.

➢ **Foster Profit and Growth**: Making informed packaging decisions will lead to tangible business outcomes, from reduced waste and lower costs to increased market share and higher profits.

## A Path to a Brighter Future for Your Brand

Ultimately, my promise is to guide you through the complexities of the packaging industry with clarity and confidence, helping you make decisions that not only protect your business but drive it toward greater success.

By selecting the right shrink-sleeve products and services, suited specifically to your needs, you'll pave the way for a future where your brand stands out and succeeds in a competitive landscape

# *Curious about the Man Behind the Promise?*

While you are attracted to the big promise I made in the previous chapter, you are also curious to know who the man behind this amazing promise is and what makes him so confident. Right?

Well, let's put that question to rest in this chapter.

I'm Shubham Singhal, the CEO of Jagannath Labels Pvt Ltd and Director of the Jagannath Group of Companies. With an MBA in Operations Management and over six years of hands-on experience in the shrink sleeves industry, I bring deep knowledge and passion to the field. My expertise comes from leading my company strategically & operationally and driving innovation and growth within the packaging sector. What is more, My experience includes the dual perspectives of not just helming my company but also working hands-on as an Operations Manager for a reputed packaging company.

My interest in plastic and packaging started when I was a child. I loved traveling and meeting new people, which helped me understand their problems and find solutions. As shared earlier, at 21, I began my career as an operations manager at a well-known packaging company in Delhi. I worked hard and, within two years, became the head of operations.

In 2019, I joined my father's business as a second-generation entrepreneur. This role allows me to use my experience in the packaging industry while continuing our family legacy.

Not one to be content with what I have learned, I believe in being a lifelong learner and enjoy attending national and international conferences on packaging, especially in the beverage industry. These experiences fuel my passion for creating unique products that people love while also making sure they are profitable for businesses.

I focus on researching market trends and what consumers want to develop exciting new designs and eco-friendly packaging. I believe sustainability is important for our future, and I try to incorporate eco-friendly practices in my work.

My team and I help both multinational and Indian FMCG companies design innovative shrink-sleeve solutions quickly and accurately. We work closely with our clients to understand their needs and ensure our products meet high quality and safety standards.  I believe in teamwork and enjoy collaborating with different people to bring our ideas to life.

As I continue to grow in my role, I am committed to pushing the limits of what's possible in packaging while ensuring we meet consumer demands and contribute positively to the environment.

Guided by the desire to serve clients and customers with my knowledge and understanding of the packaging industry, I decided to author my first book, ' 5 SECRETS TO PROFITABLE SHRINK SLEEVES.

This book reflects my commitment to sharing the transformative potential of shrink sleeve technology, drawing on my professional journey and a dedication to ongoing learning & excellence.

If you're ready to dive into the world of transformation and understanding Shrink-Sleeve Technology, let's move to the first secret which is simple yet is the foundation of success.

# CHAPTER - 1

# *#Secret: 1*

# Always Begin With The Basics Understanding Shrink Sleeves

Before achieving mastery or success in any field, it is essential to have a complete and thorough understanding of its foundational elements.

The same is true for shrink sleeves, a powerful yet often misunderstood tool in the world of packaging. To harness their full potential and unlock the competitive advantages they offer, we must first understand what shrink sleeves truly are, their different types, and how they function.

**In this chapter, we will explore these fundamentals in detail, as understanding shrink sleeves inside and out is the first secret to success in this industry.**

Only with this knowledge can you fully appreciate their transformative impact and apply them effectively in real-world scenarios.

Shrink sleeves, often referred to by various names such as shrink labels, PVC labels, or simply shrink wraps, are sometimes confusing to those unfamiliar with them. While these terms might seem different, they all describe the same product. So, let me clarify what exactly a shrink sleeve is:

> ## So, What Is A Shrink Sleeve?
>
> - A shrink sleeve is a type of label that wraps around a container and shrinks tightly when heated.
> - It's made from plastic materials like PVC or PET, and once applied to the container, it forms a snug fit by shrinking in size when exposed to heat.
> - This not only makes the label look neat and secure but also allows for full-color graphics and detailed designs.
> - Shrink sleeves are used for a variety of products, from beverages and food items to personal care goods.
> - Shrink sleeves provide both an attractive appearance and added protection against tampering.

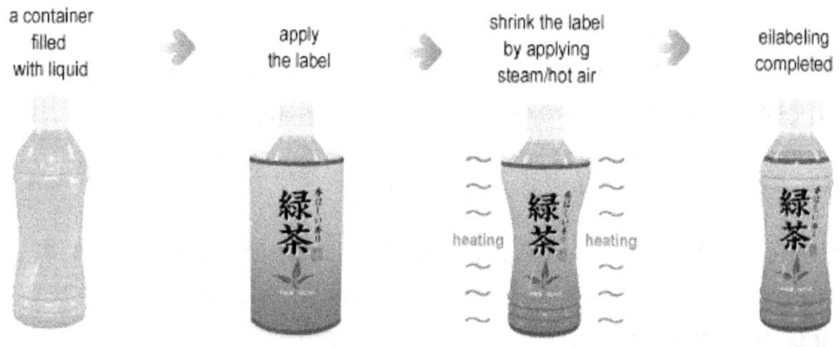


## How Shrink Sleeves Can Transform Your Brand?

Shrink sleeves can significantly enhance your brand by offering several key benefits:

1. **Eye-Catching Design:** Shrink sleeves provide 360-degree coverage of your product, allowing for vibrant, full-color graphics and intricate designs.

   **This visual appeal can make your product stand out on the shelf and attract consumer attention.**

2. **Brand Identity:** With the ability to print detailed artwork and branding elements, shrink sleeves help **reinforce your brand's identity.** Custom designs, logos, and messaging can be prominently displayed, **strengthening brand recognition and loyalty.**

3. **Product Differentiation:** Shrink sleeves can be tailored to fit unique shapes and sizes of containers, allowing for creative and distinctive packaging solutions. This customization helps differentiate your product from competitors and can enhance its perceived value.

4. **Tamper-Evident Security:** Shrink sleeves **provide a clear indication if a product has been tampered with.** This feature not only boosts consumer confidence but also **adds a layer of security to protect your brand's reputation.**

5. **Enhanced Functionality:** Shrink sleeves can **bundle multiple products together,** making them **ideal for promotions and multi-pack offers.** This functionality can increase sales and offer added convenience for consumers.

6. **Durability and Protection:** The shrink sleeve material is designed to withstand handling and environmental factors, **protecting your product** and ensuring that it arrives at the consumer in excellent condition.

## The Global Shrink Sleeve Labels Landscape

The market share of sleeves is increasing day by day, and that is because of their cost-effectiveness, providing a budget-friendly option for manufacturers and they are tamper-evident protection, which enhances product security.

➢ The Shrink Sleeve Labels Market Size was valued at USD 17.10 Billion in 2023.

➢ The Shrink Sleeve Labels industry is projected to grow from USD 18.19 Billion in 2024 to USD 28.1 Billion by 2032, exhibiting a compound annual growth rate (CAGR) of 5.58% during the forecast period (2024 - 2032).

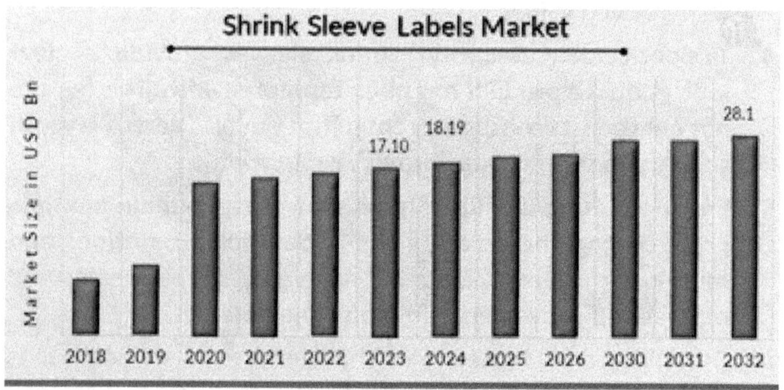


The demand for a product's shelf life to be extended is growing, and there are more stringent laws and regulations in place to prevent product tampering and counterfeiting.

These are the key market drivers enhancing the market growth of Shrink Sleeve Labels.

Now that this chapter has equipped you with a complete understanding of shrink sleeves, let's move on to the next where I will reveal to you the next secret to success and profits—developing new products.

# CHAPTER - 2

# *#Secret: 2*

# Perfecting New Product Development Step-by-Step

Developing a new shrink sleeve involves several key steps to ensure that the final product meets both functional and aesthetic requirements. However, let's begin by reviewing the current cycle of development which you are most likely following:

➢ Container development

➢ Samples for size development

➢ Trial of samples for size approval

➢ Artwork approval of approved size

➢ Cylinder development

➢ Proof approval

➢ Printing of approved artwork

➢ Supply as suggested

The steps detailed above are the most basic steps that are being followed by most of the packaging suppliers.

**However, there are additional important steps that are often missed because either suppliers may not be aware of them or you as a client are not aware of and don't ask for them.**

**Let me explain this better with an example—**

If you are a purchaser, whether a business owner or marketing manager, you know your product best and can envision the ideal packaging you want. However, it can be challenging to communicate this vision to your team or supplier. As a result, you might end up with a subpar product—such as poor colour combinations, distorted artwork due to the container shape, or misaligned elements after the sleeve shrinks.

More often than not, time constraints or pre-prepared cylinders leave you with little choice but to accept these substandard sleeves, **even when you know they don't meet your expectations.**

But I have great news for you!

You no longer have to be limited by constraints such as time or pre-pared cylinders.

Using new-age technology we can make your job super-easy and avoid all mess by using

## The Global Standard of " Perfect Sleeving Technique" - PST

Here are the steps which you should add to your new product development cycle to get perfect sleeves even if you don't have a packaging professional on your team :

## Key Line Drawing or KLD

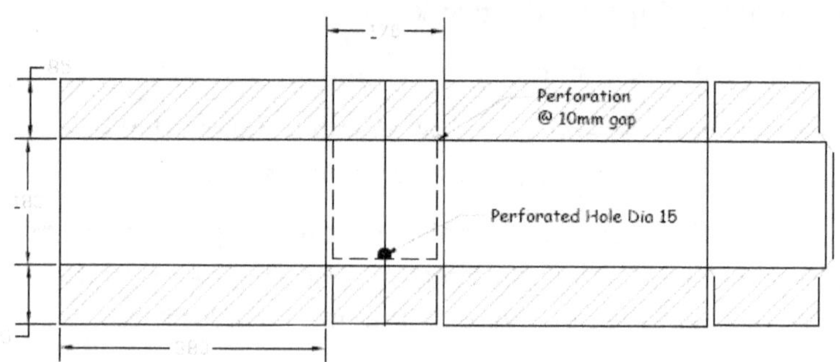

➢ **Get a KLD**

**KLD, or Key Line Drawing** is a term very commonly used by packaging professionals nowadays. Providing a KLD to your designer is crucial as it will help them to accurately align the design correctly as per the container's shape. This ensures that no design elements are hidden and that key features—such as your brand name—are prominently displayed in the main branding area of the container. By using a KLD, you can ensure that your packaging design is both aesthetically attractive and functional.

➢ **3D View**

With technology being at its best, today you can easily obtain a 3D and ARC view of your container to see how it will look after it is sleeved. This gives you an accurate preview of how your product will look on the table or shelf when it will be placed and this can be done even before production has started .

By visualizing the final design in advance, you can ensure that your packaging stands out and makes an impact in real-world settings, allowing for any necessary adjustments before moving forward with manufacturing and saving huge costs of redesigning or damage to reputation and branding by settling for sub-par packaging.

➢ **Shrinking Prediction Technology**

Using predictive software, you can now get a shrinking prediction done for your artwork. This will show you how your artwork will shrink, allowing you to adjust your design, text, and images to ensure a non-distorted appearance after sleeving. This helps you orient every element correctly, so the final product maintains the look fit and clarity you want.

## KLD & ARC To The Rescue Saving Precious Time & Lakhs of Rupees

### A CASE STUDY

**The Client:** A big and well-known Mustard Oil Manufacturer in Kota, Rajasthan, who wishes to remain anonymous for privacy reasons.

**The Problem:** The company was facing a major issue with the distortion of its brand logo on shrink sleeves. The owner was confused and frustrated because the sleeves looked unappealing once applied to the container; the logo appeared much more shrunk than intended.

**The Investigation:** Upon investigation, we learned that their current vendor could not resolve the issue because they lacked the necessary predictive technology.

**The Simple Yet Brilliant Solution:** With the help of KLD and ARC View, we provided them with a precise visualisation of how their container would look once the sleeve was applied. Additionally, using Jagannath's shrinking prediction technology, we offered them the best solution to address the distortion.

**The Transformational Results:** Our technique helped the client save lakhs of rupees and valuable time in launching their product.

As a result, for the past five years, the client has been very satisfied with our solutions, enjoying both improved product presentation and significant cost savings.

**The Takeaway:** This case clearly illustrates the value of using advanced techniques in the packaging process to avoid costly mistakes and ensure a successful product launch.

Now that you have the steps to perfect product development, it's time to move on to the next secret, as you are well aware that the success of a recipe depends on having the right ingredients. So is with Shrink Sleeves, the perfect raw material is crucial to making a great sleeve. This is what we will discover in the next secret......

☐ ☐ ☐ ☐

# CHAPTER - 3

# *#Secret: 3*

# Zeroing In On The
# Prefect Raw Material

In the world of packaging, the choice of raw materials is paramount, as it directly impacts the quality, performance, and sustainability of the final product.

**When it comes to shrink sleeves, polyvinyl chloride (PVC) has emerged as one of the most popular materials due to its unique properties and versatility.**

A variety of shrink sleeve substrates are available in the Indian market, each developed to meet specific requirements.

Throughout my career, I have encountered many companies that are aware of these different substrates, yet I have noticed that some clients use films and inks that are either over- or under-specified for their needs.

This mismatch can lead to a range of issues, including poor print quality, inadequate shrinkage, or compromised durability.

**Understanding the correct specifications for materials is crucial for achieving the best possible performance and ensuring that the final product meets both functional and aesthetic standards.**

In this chapter, we will delve into the various substrates available, their specific applications, and the importance of selecting the right materials for successful shrink-sleeve packaging.

## 1. PVC ( Polyvinyl Chloride)

**Polyvinyl Chloride (PVC) is one of the most widely used plastics in the world, known for its versatility and durability. It works with almost all shrink tunnels and container material.**

PVC is highly resistant to moisture, chemicals, and environmental factors, making it an ideal choice for protecting products during storage and transportation. Its ability to provide a tamper-evident seal adds an extra layer of security, reassuring consumers about the integrity of the product.

However, PVC has come under scrutiny due to its potential to release carcinogenic gases when burned, leading many global companies to recommend alternatives. Despite this concern, PVC is highly recyclable, provided it is properly collected and disposed of. When recycled correctly, PVC can be repurposed into new products, reducing waste and promoting sustainability.

**There are different types of PVC, each with unique properties and applications.**

➤ **CAST or Calender PVC** is a superior quality of PVC and is used in unevenly shaped containers where printing is very complex.

➤ **Blown PVC** is a cheaper version - that is easily available and widely used in the market as an alternative to CAST PVC.

## 2. PETG ( Polyethylene Terephthalate Glycol )

PETG, or Polyethylene Terephthalate Glycol-Modified, is a thermoplastic polymer that is an excellent choice for a variety of applications, particularly in packaging.

PETG was developed as a replacement for PVC, which releases carcinogenic gases when burned and has low recycling rates. Many companies have transitioned from PVC to PETG for these reasons. However, not all PVC sleeves can be replaced with PETG due to certain limitations—PETG may not be compatible with specific container materials, making it

PETG works perfectly in steam tunnels but faces challenges when used in hot air tunnels,  with HDPE or  PP containers. The heat distribution in hot air tunnels can make it difficult for PETG sleeves to shrink properly on these materials, limiting their effectiveness in certain applications.

## 3. OPS ( Oriented Polystyrene)

Oriented Polystyrene (OPS) was developed in Japan as an alternative to PVC, primarily due to environmental concerns associated with PVC production and disposal. OPS has gained popularity across various industries, including food service, cosmetics, and retail, thanks to its advantageous properties such as strength, clarity, and lightweight design.

**However, the cost of OPS is relatively high due to a limited number of manufacturers and the requirement for permanent refrigeration throughout all stages of production and transportation.**

This additional logistical challenge can drive up costs.

Moreover, OPS is often preferred for exports to Japan, where it is considered a local product and is more readily accepted by consumers and businesses alike. Its alignment with

Japanese standards and preferences further boosts its appeal in the market.

**As demand for sustainable packaging solutions continues to grow, OPS remains a notable choice for companies seeking environmentally friendly options, despite its higher production costs.**

## Selection of Inks

Inks are a crucial component of shrink sleeves, playing a vital role in both functionality and aesthetics.

**The choice of ink can significantly affect the visual appeal of the packaging, as well as its performance characteristics.**

**Most Printers, however, don't pay much attention to this most important piece of raw material and end up creating a sub-standard sleeve.**

The key to a **world-class** Shrik Sleeve lies not **only** in choosing a **suitable** base material but the right ink— Shrinkable Ink:

---

### So, What Are Shrinkable Inks?

- Shrinkable inks are specialised inks designed for use on shrink sleeves and labels.

- When heated, these inks can contract along with the substrate, ensuring that the printed design maintains its integrity and visual appeal during the shrinking process.

- This characteristic is particularly important in applications where the sleeve needs to fit snugly around a product, such as bottles, jars, and containers.

---

Incorporating shrinkable inks and PVC into packaging designs is essential for achieving high-quality, visually appealing products that meet consumer expectations. By choosing the right type of material, brands can enhance their packaging effectiveness while ensuring that their printed designs maintain integrity during the shrinking process.

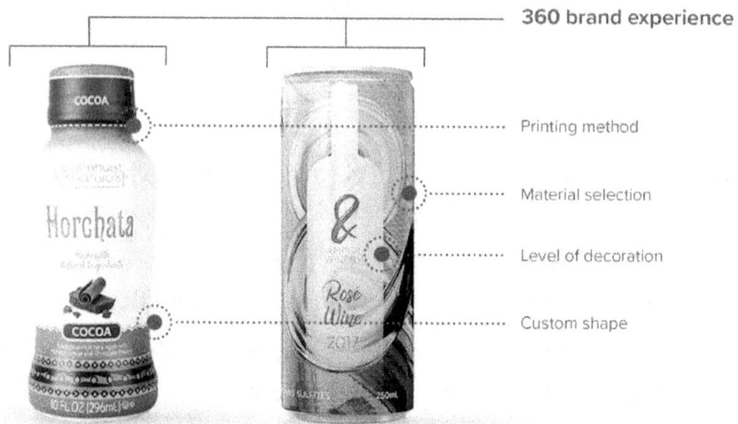


The next chapter will reveal a secret that is bigger in perspective and impact than the rest as it is the key not just to profitable shrink-sleeves but to creating and sustaining your entire brand.

# CHAPTER - 4

# *#Secret: 4*

# Leveraging The Power Of Artwork & A Perfect Logo

In this chapter, let's talk about a component that is not only crucial for creating an effective shrink sleeve but is key to creating a successful and profitable brand— your Logo!

A well-designed logo and packaging are essential for building a brand, especially in the competitive packaging industry.

Your logo & your packaging are the first to interact with your consumers even before your product. They make a strong first impression on consumers, showing that the brand is professional and trustworthy, which can influence buying decisions.

**A good logo represents the company's values and helps people recognize and remember the brand.**

In a crowded market, a unique logo sets a brand apart from its competitors, encouraging customer loyalty. Effective design also connects with emotions, making it easier for consumers to relate to the brand. Consistent use of a logo and design across all products helps reinforce brand identity and trust.

Additionally, a versatile logo looks good on various packaging types, ensuring it remains appealing. Eye-catching designs improve marketing efforts, attracting attention and encouraging engagement. Overall, investing in a high-quality logo and design is important for creating a successful and lasting brand.

## 8 Steps to Create the Best Design and Logo

Creating an impactful logo and design is a vital process that can significantly influence how your brand is perceived.

Here's a detailed guide with eight essential steps to help you craft a logo that connects with your audience and effectively represents your brand.

1.  **Understand Your Brand**: The first step in designing an effective logo is to thoroughly understand your brand. Reflect on your brand's core values, mission, and the message you want to convey. Consider your target audience and what they value. Are you aiming for a playful, modern look, or something more traditional and sophisticated? This clarity will serve as a foundation for all your design decisions, ensuring that your logo aligns with your brand's identity and resonates with the intended audience.

2.  **Research and Gather Inspiration**: Conduct research to explore logos and designs within your industry as well as outside of it. Look at competitors to identify trends, strengths, and weaknesses in their branding. Gather inspiration from various sources, such as design websites, social media platforms, and nature. Create a mood board that visually captures elements you like—this can include colours, shapes, and styles. This research phase not only helps you identify what works but also inspires innovative ideas that can set your brand apart.

3.  **Choose Colors and Fonts Wisely**: Colors and fonts are crucial components of your logo. Each color evokes different emotions and associations, so choose hues that align with your brand's personality. For example, blue often represents trust and professionalism, while green conveys growth and sustainability. Similarly, select fonts that reflect your brand's tone—serif fonts can convey tradition and reliability, while

sans-serif fonts may suggest modernity and simplicity. Consistency in these elements is essential for building a cohesive brand identity.

4. **Sketch Ideas**: Once you have a clear understanding of your brand and some inspiration, start sketching out your logo ideas. This stage is about free expression—don't worry about perfection. Draw multiple concepts, exploring different shapes, layouts, and symbols. This brainstorming process allows for creativity to flow without the constraints of digital tools. Aim for a diverse range of ideas, and don't hesitate to mix and match elements from different sketches to create something unique.

5. **Create Digital Drafts**: After selecting the most promising sketches, transition to digital design. Use design software like Adobe Illustrator or Canva to create digital versions of your logos. This step allows you to refine your concepts, experiment with color palettes, and adjust typography. Pay attention to the balance and alignment of elements, ensuring that your logo is visually appealing and harmonious. This is the stage where your ideas begin to take shape in a more polished form.

6. **Seek Feedback**: With several digital drafts in hand, it's time to gather feedback. Share your designs with trusted colleagues, friends, or members of your target audience. Encourage honest and constructive criticism—ask specific questions about what resonates and what doesn't. Understanding how others perceive your logo is invaluable, as it may highlight aspects you hadn't considered. Use this feedback to make informed adjustments to your design, enhancing its effectiveness.

7. **Test Across Different Applications**: A great logo should be versatile and work well across various mediums. Test your

logo in different formats, such as business cards, websites, social media profiles, and packaging. Ensure it remains clear and visually appealing, whether it's displayed in color or black and white. Consider how it looks at various sizes, from large banners to small icons. This testing phase helps ensure that your logo maintains its integrity and impact regardless of where it appears.

8.  **Refine and Finalize**: Based on the feedback and testing, take the time to refine your design. Make any necessary adjustments to ensure it meets your brand's needs and effectively communicates your message. Consider elements like spacing, color consistency, and overall balance. Once you're satisfied with the final design, prepare the logo in various file formats for different uses (e.g., PNG, JPEG, SVG). This finalization process is crucial for ensuring your logo is ready for implementation across all branding materials.

By following these eight comprehensive steps, you can create a logo and design that authentically represents your brand and resonates with your target audience. A well-crafted logo not only enhances brand recognition but also helps establish a lasting connection with consumers.

The Importance of Logo Design in Branding Strategy

## How Our Logo Transformed Our Business

Before I entered our business, our logo was very simple and created quickly without much thought. After attending several international conferences and reading extensively about branding and design, I realized the importance of having a strong logo.

We decided to redesign our logo, focusing on how colors impact perception.

For instance, we learned that switching our logo from white and blue to blue and white—similar to many successful brands—could make a significant difference.

This small change greatly improved how customers viewed us.

By investing time and effort into our logo and understanding colour psychology, we transformed our brand image and strengthened our connection with our audience. This experience taught me that a well-thought-out logo is crucial for any business.

In just five years, our work has doubled, and we are growing rapidly. This change in our branding played a key role in our success.

**Old Logo**

**New Logo**

No business or process is complete unless it adheres to regulatory compliance and that my dear readers is the 5th profitable shrink-sleeve secret that I am about to reveal in the next chapter.

□ □ □ □

# CHAPTER - 5

# *#Secret: 5*

# Ensuring Compliance Perfect Knowledge of Government Rules for Packaging

Compliance with regulatory guidelines is a huge part of any business's success, as is the case with shrink sleeves.

In order to guarantee safety, businesses in India must ensure sustainability, and consumer protection by following the regulatory guidelines for packaging.

The main areas of emphasis are governed by the following—

1.  **The Food Safety and Standards Authority of India (FSSAI)**

    - F&B packaging materials are under control by the FSSAI. Packaging has to be safe, clean, and non-toxic.

    - It calls for labeling standards covering component lists, nutritional data, and allergen warnings.

    - Packaging has to also show the "best before" date.

2.  **The Bureau of Indian Standards (BIS)**

    - The BIS defines criteria of quality for several packaging materials. Following these criteria guarantees the dependability and safety of products.

    - Some products, particularly in consumer goods and electronics, can call for specific BIS certification.

3.  **Rules for Plastic Waste Management**

    - These guidelines seek to lower plastic waste and advance environmentally friendly living.

    - Plastic product producers and importers have to control waste by means of collecting and recycling.

    - The regulations also prohibit some single-use plastics and, wherever feasible, demand the use of biodegradable substitutes.

4.  **The Packaging Waste Management Protocol**

    - Under the Extended Producer Responsibility (EPR) framework manufacturers have to take responsibility for the complete lifecycle of their packaging including post-consumer waste management.

    - Businesses have to have strategies for gathering and reusing packaging materials in order to reduce environmental effects.

### 5. The Environment Protection Act

- Hazardous chemical usage in packaging is controlled under this statute. Businesses have to guarantee that their packaging materials follow relevant environmental criteria and do not damage the surroundings.

### 6. Labelling & Consumer Protection

- The Legal Metrology Act mandates precise and explicit labelling of packaged goods including weight, volume, and price, therefore addressing consumer protection.

- Misleading information is strictly forbidden; companies have to make sure any claims on packaging are supported by facts.

### 7. Chemicals (Management and Safety) Guidelines

- These guidelines control chemical use in packaging materials. Businesses have to make sure that dangerous substances from their packaging don't seep or leach into goods.

Understanding and following these rules helps Indian companies guarantee compliance, safeguard customer health, and support environmentally friendly packaging methods. Further improving compliance efforts is keeping current on changes in rules and interacting with trade associations.

> ### Enhancing Environmental Practices Ensured Inspection Clearance & Saved Lahks in Fines & Avoided a 30-Day Factory Closure
>
> I have a client in Agra with a strong market presence. I met the owners at a conference through a mutual friend, and they invited me to visit their plant.

During my visit, I was impressed by their operations but noticed they **were improperly disposing of some wastewater, which could harm the environment.**

**I offered suggestions for improving their waste disposal practices, and they took my advice seriously.**

A few months later, one of the owners, Mr. Aditya called to share some great news during a recent inspection, **government officials visited their plant and found it compliant with waste disposal regulations—one of only two plants out of over 20 checked.**

**They saved around 15 lakh in potential fines and avoided a 30-day factory closure. Mr. Aditya was thrilled with the results!**

This experience highlighted the importance of addressing environmental issues early and the positive impact of collaboration.

Within the following pages is the proof of the results that come from following these 5 profitable shrink-sleeve secrets that I have shared above.

# EXPRESSIONS OF ENDORSEMENT & GRATITUDE FROM CLIENTS

**Ankit Bhangadiya**

Bhangadiya Beverages, Ajmer, Rajasthan

"I had many packaging problems that were hurting my business. After working with Shubham, I can say they are all solved! They gave me helpful advice and made our shrink-sleeve packaging much better.

Now, the quality is great, and my sales have increased. I'm really thankful for their help and highly recommend their services!"

---

**Ramdev Vyas**

Ramdev Agencies, Jodhpur, Rajasthan

"I want to thank Shubham for helping us with our shrink-sleeve packaging. We had big problems because the sleeves didn't fit right, and this hurt our sales. I felt lost trying to fix it.

When I talked to Shubham, he listened to my issues and really understood what we needed. They gave us good advice and helped us find the right materials.

After we made their changes, our sleeves fit perfectly! **Our products look great now, and our sales have gone up 30%."**

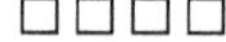

# Together Let's Impact
# The Packaging World Positively

As we come to the end of this book, I want to thank you for learning about shrink sleeves and packaging with me. I am sure the secrets shared here will help you make better choices for your business. Whether you have a lot of experience or are just starting out, making the right decisions can lead to success.

The packaging industry is always changing, so it's important to stay curious and open to new ideas. I encourage you to use what you've learned in your own work. Together, we can make a positive difference.

If you have any questions or need help, just scan the QR code to book a time with me. Fill out the form, and I'll set up the next available slot for you.

Thank you for being part of this journey, and I wish you all the best in the future